jazz tracks for [...]

Arranged by Steve Rawlins

CONTENTS

On the CD:
Steve Rawlins, piano; Jim DeJulio, bass;
Gordon Peeke, drums; Steve Rawlins, producer;
Andy Waterman, engineer

ISBN 978-0-634-06069-4

This publication is not for sale in the EU.

HAL•LEONARD®
CORPORATION
7777 W. BLUEMOUND RD. P.O. BOX 13819 MILWAUKEE, WI 53213

Visit Hal Leonard Online at
www.HalLeonard.com

The chords below the line are the traditional harmonies. The chords above the line are
more advanced, alternate harmonies. The trio recordings use both versions variously.
The deliberately low keys will suit most women who sing jazz.

Come Rain or Come Shine

WOMEN'S KEY

FROM ST. LOUIS WOMAN

WORDS BY JOHNNY MERCER
MUSIC BY HAROLD ARLEN

SLOW BLUES FEEL

(2ND TIME INSTRUMENTAL SOLO

I'm gon-na love you like no-bod-y's loved you, come rain or come shine.

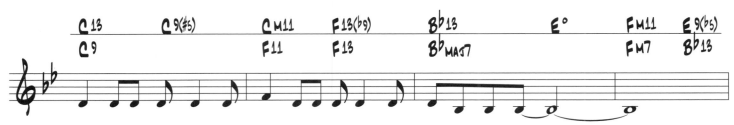

High as a moun-tain and deep as a riv-er, come rain or come shine.

(2ND TIME VOCAL RETURNS

I guess when you met me it was just one of those things,

but don't ev-er bet me 'cause I'm gon-na be true if you let me.

3

Do Nothin' Till You Hear From Me

Women's Key

Words and Music by Duke Ellington
and Bob Russell

Moderately Slow Swing

The Frim Fram Sauce

Women's Key

Words and music by Joe Ricardel
and Redd Evans

Easy Swing

Good Morning Heartache

WOMEN'S KEY

WORDS AND MUSIC BY DAN FISHER,
IRENE HIGGINBOTHAM AND ERVIN DRAKE

SLOW BLUES TEMPO

Black Coffee

Women's Key

Words and Music by Paul Francis Webster
and Sonny Burke

Slow and Bluesy

(2X Instrumental Solo

A

feel-in' might-y lone-some, have-n't slept a wink, I walk the floor and watch the door and in bet-ween I drink black

cof - fee._____ Love's a hand - me - down broom._____ I'll

(2nd Time Improvise Vocal, Light Hum

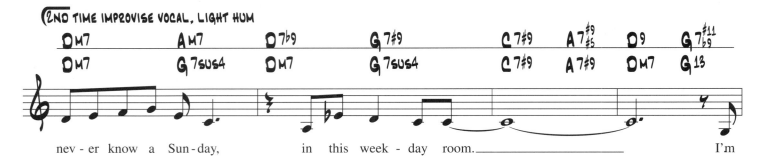

nev - er know a Sun-day, in this week - day room._____ I'm

B

talk-in' to the shad-ows, one o'-clock to four. and Lord, how slow the mo-ments go when all I do is pour black

Hello, Young Lovers

FROM THE KING AND I

Women's Key

Jazz Waltz

Lyrics by Oscar Hammerstein II
Music by Richard Rodgers

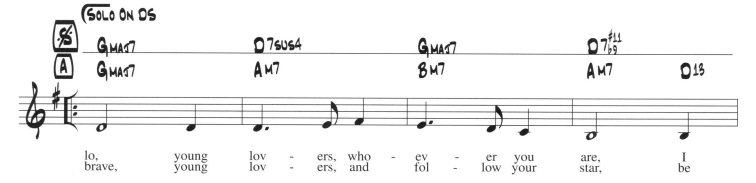

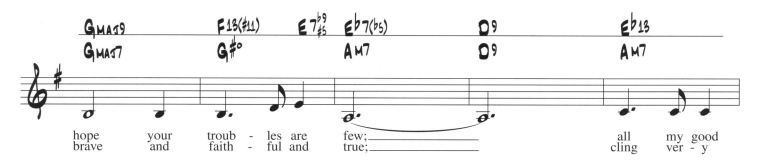

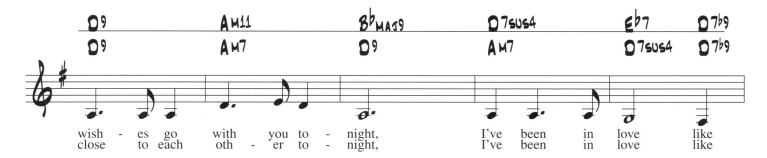

14

Honeysuckle Rose

FROM AIN'T MISBEHAVIN'

Women's Key

Words by Andy Razaf
Music by Thomas "Fats" Waller

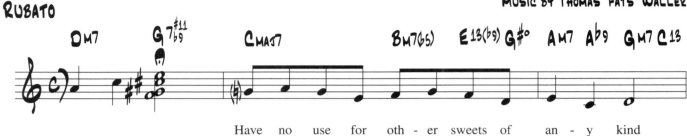

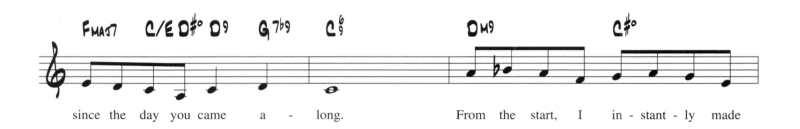

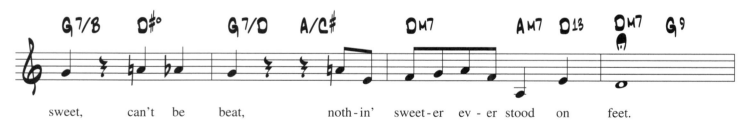

Easy Swing

My Funny Valentine

FROM BABES IN ARMS

Women's Key

Words by Lorenz Hart
Music by Richard Rodgers

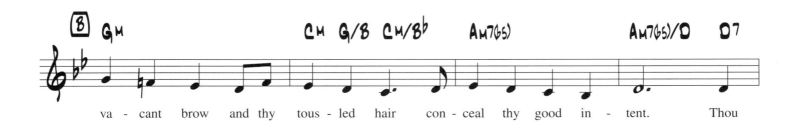

21

I'm Beginning To See The Light

Women's Key

Words And Music By Don George, Johnny Hodges, Duke Ellington And Harry James

Swing

(2nd time Vocal scat

nev-er cared much for moon-lit skies,___ I nev-er wink back at fire-flies,___ but

now that the stars are in your eyes,___ I'm be-gin-ning to see the light.___ I

nev-er went in for af-ter glow,___ or can-dle-light on the mis-tle-toe,___ but

now when you turn the lamp down low,___ I'm be-gin-ning to see the light.___

(2nd time Vocal words Returns

Used to ram-ble thru the park,___ shad-ow box-ing in the dark.___

23

Lost Mind

Women's Key

Words and Music by Percy Mayfield

'Round Midnight

Women's Key

Words by Bernie Hanighen
Music by Thelonious Monk and Cootie Williams

Moderately slow, in 2

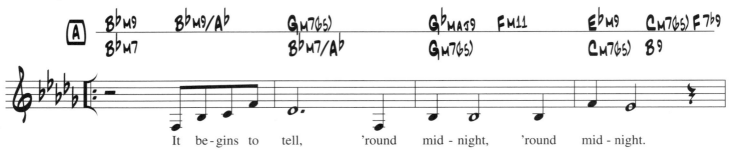

(2ND TIME LIGHT VOCAL IMPROVISATION ON "OOH"

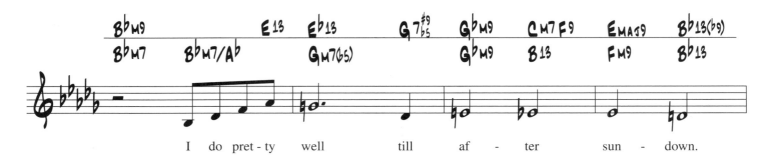

It be-gins to tell, 'round mid-night, 'round mid-night.

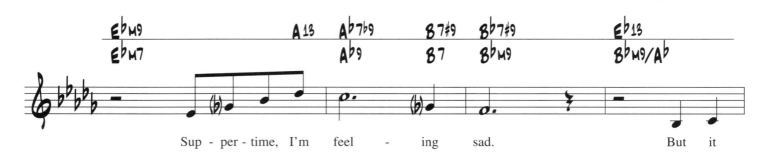

I do pret-ty well till af-ter sun-down.

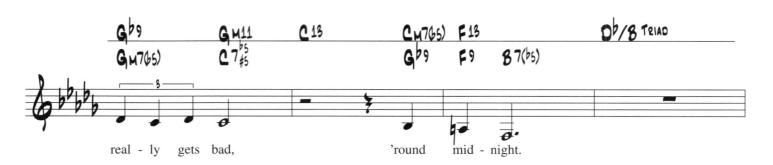

Sup-per-time, I'm feel-ing sad. But it

real-ly gets bad, 'round mid-night.

Route 66

Women's Key

By Bobby Troup

make that Cal - i - for - nia trip.___ Get your

kicks   on Route_ Six - ty - Six!___   (If   you)_

Get   your   kicks   on   Route_   Six - ty - Six!_

Get   your   kicks   on   Route_   Six - ty - Six!_

Skylark

Women's Key

Words by Johnny Mercer
Music by Hoagy Carmichael

Moderately

(2nd time instrumental solo or light vocal improv.

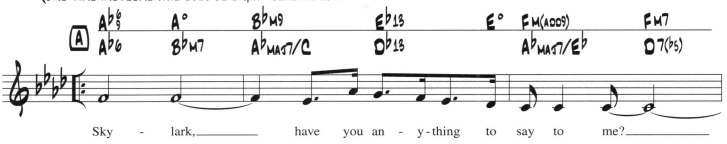

Sky - lark,_____ have you an - y-thing to say to me?_____

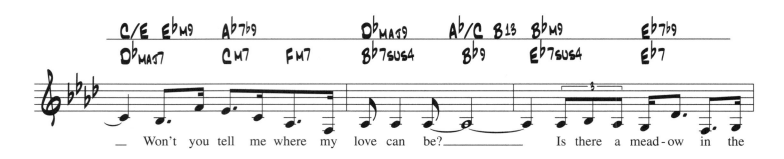

_ Won't you tell me where my love can be?_____ Is there a mead-ow in the

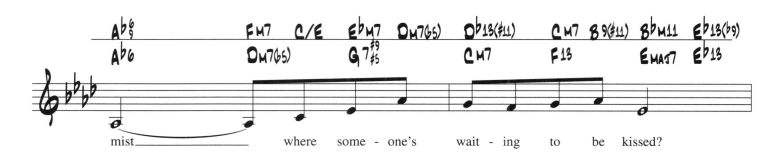

mist_____ where some - one's wait - ing to be kissed?

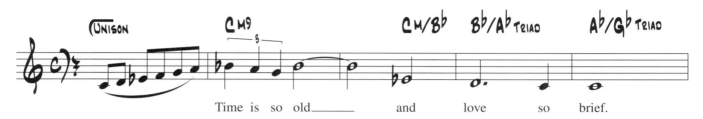

Speak Low

FROM THE MUSICAL PRODUCTION ONE TOUCH OF VENUS

WOMEN'S KEY

WORDS BY OGDEN NASH
MUSIC BY KURT WEILL

You've Changed

Women's Key

Words and Music by Bill Carey
and Carl Fischer

MORE VOCAL COLLECTIONS
STANDARDS

FROM HAL•LEONARD®

JAZZ VOCAL STANDARDS

Transcriptions of Landmark Arrangements
This outstanding collection assembles and transcribes for piano and voice 18 of the finest recordings in the world of singing. Featured are such legends as: Louis Armstrong ("Ain't Misbehavin'"), Ray Charles ("Georgia on My Mind"), Nat "King" Cole ("Route 66"), Blossom Dearie ("Peel Me a Grape"), Ella Fitzgerald ("Midnight Sun"), Billie Holiday ("Crazy He Calls Me"), Shirley Horn ("Wild Is the Wind"), Frank Sinatra ("I've Got You Under My Skin"), Sarah Vaughan ("An Occasional Man"), and many more. Includes a discography, and notes on each selection.
00310663 Piano/Vocal $19.95

STANDARD BALLADS

These books feature fantastic American standards in new arrangements designed to flatter any singer, with interesting harmonies and accompaniments. The arrangements are in the spirit of the performance tradition of great standards established by singers such as Tony Bennett, Rosemary Clooney, Frank Sinatra, Nat King Cole and Peggy Lee. Keys have been carefully chosen and will be comfortable for most voices. The books contain arrangements for voice and piano accompaniments, and a section of "fake book"-style editions of the arrangements convenient for performing. The companion CD includes wonderful performances of each song by a singer backed by piano, bass and drums, as well as trio accompaniment tracks only for practice or performance.
Songs: All the Things You Are • Autumn Leaves • Call Me Irresponsible • East of the Sun (And West of the Moon) • I Left My Heart in San Francisco • I'll Be Seeing You • In a Sentimental Mood • Isn't It Romantic • The Very Thought of You • The Way You Look Tonight.
00740088 Women's Edition $19.95
00740089 Men's Edition $19.95

TORCH SONGS — WOMEN'S EDITION

The Singer's Series

Fantastic heart-on-the-sleeve American standards in new arrangements designed to flatter any singer, with interesting harmonies and accompaniments. The arrangements are in the spirit of the performance tradition established by singers such as Judy Garland, Tony Bennett, Frank Sinatra, Nat King Cole, Peggy Lee and others. Keys have been carefully chosen and will be comfortable for most voices. The book contains arrangements for voice and piano accompaniment, plus a section of "fake book"-style arrangements convenient for performing. The accompanying CD includes great performances of each song by a singer backed by piano, bass and drums, as well as trio acompaniment tracks only for practice or performance.
00740086 Book/CD Pack $19.95

TORCH SONGS — MEN'S EDITION

The Singer's Series

Great singer/trio arrangements in comfortable singing keys. The Women's Edition includes: Bewitched • Cry Me a River • I Can't Get Started with You • The Man That Got Away • Misty • More Than You Know • My Foolish Heart • My Man (Mon Homme) • Stormy Weather (Keeps Rainin' All the Time) • When the Sun Comes Out. Men's Edition includes: Angel Eyes • Bewitched • Blame It on My Youth • Here's That Rainy Day • I Can't Get Started with You • In the Wee Small Hours of the Morning • Memories of You • Misty • More Than You Know • One for My Baby (And One More for the Road).
00740087 Book/CD Pack $19.95